T0131467

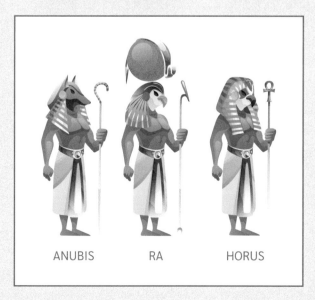

ANUBIS   RA   HORUS

THE
CREATION
OF
GODS
AND
RELIGIONS

A SIMPLE EXPLANATION

Miguel Rosado

Archway Publishing books may be ordered through booksellers or by contacting:

Archway Publishing
1663 Liberty Drive
Bloomington, IN 47403
www.archwaypublishing.com
844-669-3957

ISBN: 978-1-6657-0689-6 (sc)
ISBN: 978-1-6657-0690-2 (hc)
ISBN: 978-1-6657-0691-9 (e)

Library of Congress Control Number: 2021909628

Print information available on the last page.

Archway Publishing rev. date: 7/1/2021

Is there is a God?
Do I need a religion or God?
Why are there so many religions?

Let's take a
journey into
these questions.

There was a time when our human ancestors did not have written languages or schools. It took humanity thousands of years to learn all those things that we know today.

Everything was a mystery to the early humans. They did not understand the forces of nature. They wondered what caused the blowing of the wind, the rain, volcanoes, earthquakes, lightning, the sun, the moon, for example.

DEMETER | CERES

The people started to believe that the forces of nature were caused by gods or spirits of great power. They started worshiping the sun god, wind god, fire god, volcano god, god of lightning, rain god, and many other gods.

You probably have watched movies based on many mythological gods. Those that you may call superheroes today were at their time real gods for those societies.

3

People created rituals and ceremonies to communicate with their gods for help, protection, or forgiveness or to give praise.

There is evidence that they performed dances to bring rain, offerings and sacrifices to appease an erupting volcano, ceremonies to give thanks to the sun for rising and bringing light and to the moon for illuminating the night, and many more rituals.

There is some evidence of the use of drugs during ancient ceremonies. Drugs can cause hallucinations and spiritual experiences. What influence they might have had in the creations of the gods is unknown.

As people started to understand the forces of nature, they stopped believing that they were caused by gods. People started to think of god as an invisible force, the creator of all things, so they worshipped fewer gods.

At the end, most cultures settled with one nonmaterial god, but with a few disagreements about who that god was or is. There are still some religions that have many gods.

A negative force called the "devil" plays an important role in the battle of good versus bad in many religions. Did God give the evil his power? Can he take it away?

African gods

Egyptian gods.

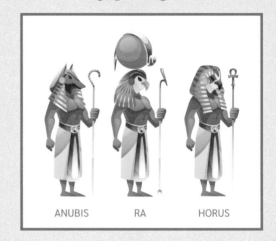

Chinese god.

There have been many gods that are no longer gods because people stopped believing in them.

Greek gods.

Slavic gods.

Ganesh.

Jesus.

Siddhidatri.

Flying spaghetti monster.

There are still many gods, but the one you are more likely to believe in is the one your family passed down to you.

Indian gods.

SHIVA   IGNY   VISHNU   YAMA

SOMA   BRAHMA   INDRA   GANESHA   SURYA

7

Our ancestors did not have much knowledge of medicine or a good understanding of how the body works. They learned to use plants and minerals to cure illnesses. The persons who learned the uses of medical plants to cure people became very important because they had *the power to cure!* They became the healers of their communities.

Once the healers began to lead the rituals and ceremonies to the gods, they ascended to positions of power in their communities. They refined the ceremonies and created elaborate costumes and practices that eventually became religious rituals in their communities.

Some healers claimed that their power was given by the gods, and some even deceived people into believing that they were gods themselves.

We can still find these practices in the traditional healers of South Africa.

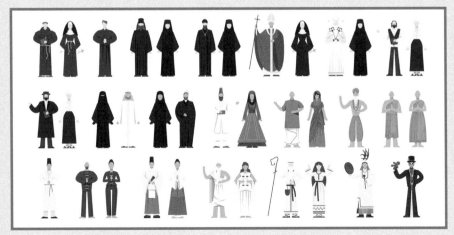

As more religions developed, conflict started. The religious leaders were competing for the same people to attract to their religion, so they fought each other. Sometimes they invaded other lands to expand their beliefs.

There have been many battles and wars fought because each religion thinks of itself as the true and only one with the right god.

Some kings and queens claimed to be gods or descendants of god, which gave them absolute power over people.

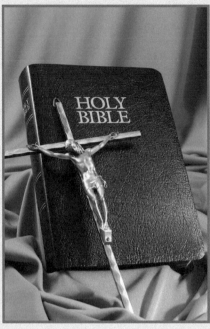
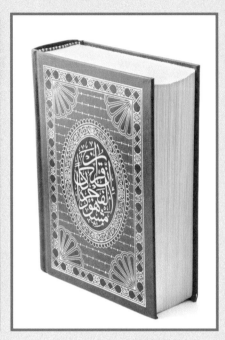

Religious institutions developed their own sacred books outlining the stories of their gods and cultures.

During those times, only privileged people could read and write. The religious leaders had power over people because they were of the few who could read the books that they proclaimed to be the words of their god.

The books mandated that the people made offerings to god, so the religious leaders became rich and powerful.

Society uses religion and spirituality to pass down to its children the moral values that the community holds. Religion can be a comforting practice for many.

You probably already were brought up in a religion. You probably accepted everything that you were told about your religion.

It is important that you analyze your beliefs and ask those questions you may have. Listen to other points of view on everything that you have accepted as true.

Following a religion out of fear or deception will not benefit you. Learning is the best weapon to fight the fear and deceptions. Some people and organizations may try to keep you from learning. Knowledge gives you power, and the more power you gain, the less they have.

Today there are thousands of religions practiced around the world. You should study them and choose whichever makes more sense to you, but you must understand that not having a religion is okay too. There are many good people who do not follow any religion.

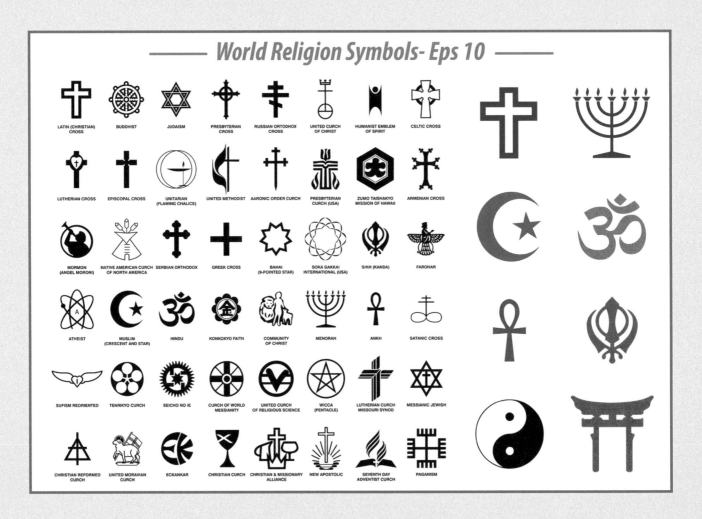

World religion symbols.

Some people proclaim that they are spiritual and not religious; they use different venues to practice their spirituality. New religions are being formed along this line and range from the mystics to the wackos. Believers, beware.

When imagination is used to create in the material world, it is called genius. When it is used to create immaterial worlds, it is called religion.

It is undeniable that religions have made good contributions to society in the areas of architecture, the arts, music, literature, and social changes, but the price paid was too high.

Horrendous acts have been committed in the name of religion: human sacrifices, the Crusades, the Thuggee murders, the Inquisition, burning of witches, condonation of slavery, child abuse, native culture destruction, and many more.

You must look at the history and determine if the path to reach a god that lives in your mind is the way of religion. Are you willing to pay the price?

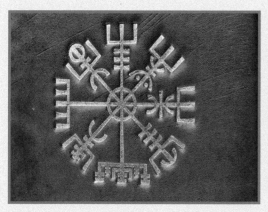  

Beware of cults. Cults are relatively small groups under a strong leader who uses religious beliefs to control the group. There are a few large cults. Cults usually end with the enrichment of the leader, sexual abuse, murder, or mass suicide.

A quick internet search of a specific group will help you determine if it is a cult. These are some indicators: Do they try to isolate you from friends and family? Do they control your time, finances, and movement? Do they administer physical punishment? Does the leader act like a dictator or a god? These are clues that it is a cult. Don't get brainwashed by their beliefs.

The monotheist religions of today believe in an all-knowing, all-powerful, loving god as the creator of everything in existence. Their religious followers do not seem to comprehend this concept because they are willing to commit terrorist acts and other injustices in the name of their god.

If we are living in the creation of a benevolent god, we should respect and care for all of its creation, not just the people.

If we are *not* living in the creation of a benevolent god, we should respect and care for everything so as not to break the balance of nature.

Most religions have an apocalyptic view of the world (end-times, Armageddon, etc.). These apocalyptic views have been around for thousands of years; so far, every one of those predictions has been a farce, and the ones that are still around are used to scare people into religion.

Religion is regarded by the common people as true, by the wise as false, and by the rulers as useful. (Lucius Annaeus Seneca)

Advances in the sciences make the way we think about god and religion an evolving process. How much is going to change during your generation? Nobody knows.

The Sun and planets of the Solar System

Sun Mercury Venus Earth Mars Jupiter Saturn Uranus Neptune

Science has answered many of our questions about nature and the universe. Science is the best tool we have to seek knowledge and understanding. Religions are attacking the sciences because they have disproved many claims of their holy books.

Science has proven that the Earth is not flat and that it is a small planet, along with other planets, revolving around the sun. Our solar system is rotating inside a galaxy that is spinning in an infinite ocean of galaxies that were formed billions of years ago.

Science has proven how humans have evolved to our present state, figured out how our brains work, provided us with cures for our diseases, and shown us how a virus kills.

The antagonistic view of some religions toward science is of great concern. Everything around you that is making your life safer, healthier, easier, richer, and more secure was made possible by science and not by religions.

If we are going to continue progressing, we must find a balance to accommodate religions without putting constraints on science and give our support to the separation of church and state.

If you are confused and seeking guidance to find the right belief system for yourself, there is one other option available to you. The Roman emperor Marcus Aurelius gave us a blueprint of how to live a just life by means of his personal writing called *Meditations*.

Here is his take on the issue of gods:

Live a good life. If there are gods and they are just, then they will not care how devout you have been but will welcome you based on the virtues you have lived by. If there are gods, but unjust, then you should not want to worship them. If there are no gods, then you will be gone, but will have lived a noble life that will live on in the memories of your loved ones. (Marcus Aurelius)

The truth is that we as people disagree when it comes to religions and the concept of god. Some people are very sure that there is a god, others are very sure that there is no god, and others are not sure what to believe.

What we can say for sure is that religions were made by men. Religions have been used for bad purposes disguised as the mandates of god and have been used for good to get grace from god.

Good people do the right thing because it is the right thing to do. It doesn't take extraordinary beliefs to be a good person.

The world is yours to understand. Learn how to reason, and use that capability to form your own belief. Think so you can be free.

ILLUSTRATIONS CREDITS

GandR01.jpg 298-20-21 © Fitzwilliam Museum | University of Cambridge The Ancient of Days
GandR02.jpg ID 110127463 © Mosprofs | Dreamstime.com Slavs ritual
GandR03.jpg ID 85343103 © Denis Belitskiy | Dreamstime.com Milky Way. Night sky
GandR04.jpg ID 65815772 © Dannyphoto80 | Dreamstime.com Caveman2
GandR05.jpg ID 124029131 © Ig0rzh | Dreamstime.com Lightning
GandR06.jpg ID 34643380 © Ig0rzh | Dreamstime.com Waterspout
GandR07.jpg ID 178216881 © Seahorse vector | Dreamstime.com Volcano eruption
GandR08.jpg ID 95234374 © Macrovector | Dreamstime.com Primal tribe people
GandR09.jpg ID 13545956 © Maen Zayyad | Dreamstime.com Bowing to the eclipse of the sun
GandR10.jpg ID 178684949 © Ratpack2 | Dreamstime.com Erectus tribe hunting
GandR11.jpg ID 25442547 © Ensiferrum | Dreamstime.com Tribal priest (shaman) conjuring above fire
GandR12.jpg ID 151421439 © Ernest Akayeu | Dreamstime.com Demeter goddess of harvest
GandR13.jpg ID 165824974 © Quicksilver77 | Dramstime.com Zeus Wrath
GandR14.jpg ID 28422857 © Felix Laflamme | Dreamstime.com Poseidon
GandR15.jpg ID 58943822 © Estelle30 | Dreamstime.com Native American gods
GandR16.jpg ID 118773153 © Iuliia Poliudova | Dreamstime.com African dancer
GandR17.jpg ID 153352091 © Ruddy Irawan | Dreamstime.com animal sacrifice
GandR18.jpg ID 134631306 © Fredweiss | Dreamstime.com native American dancing
GandR19.jpg ID 19519360 © Dave Bredeson | Dreamstime.com Girl's hands praying
GandR20.jpg ID 134712692 © Valeriy Kachaev | Dreamstime.com Prayer man
GandR21.jpg ID 93027245 © Vgorbash | Dreamstime.com Eyes-Hands mason
GandR22.jpg ID 70118803 © Danilo Sanino | Dreamstime.com Sarasvati Hindu goddess
GandR23.jpg ID 177203678 © Armi1961 | Dreamstime.com Devils play the fiddle
GandR24.jpg ID 52102902 © Estelle30 | Dreamstime.com African gods
GandR25.jpg ID 165000643 © Idey | Dreamstime.com Three Egyptian gods
GandR26.jpg ID 77763823 © Sornchai Hempolchom | Dreamstime.com Kwnao Chinese god
GandR27.jpg ID 123443479 © Tatyana Merkusheva | Dreamstime.com Greek gods
GandR28.jpg ID 79316951 © Girnyk | Dreamstime.com Veles, Perun, and Lada Slavic gods
GandR29.jpg ID 9078184 © José Marafona | Dreamstime.com Jesus
GandR30.jpg ID 4961112 © Ram Kumar | Dreamstime.com Ganesh at temple
GandR31.jpg ID 96467551 © | Dreamstime.com Flying spaghetti monster
GandR32.jpg ID 146154424 © Evgenii Naumov | Dreamstime.com Indian gods
GandR33.jpg ID 147381551 © Prabir Bahattacharjee | Dreamstime.com Siddhidatri
GandR34.jpg ID 86582920 © Philcold | Dreamstime.com Healing ritual

ILLUSTRATIONS CREDITS

GandR35.jpg ID 180236471 © Volodymyr Polotovskyi | Dreamstime.com Wild tribe Indians

GandR36.jpg ID 36360329 © Valeria Sangiovanni | Dreamstime.com African shaman's dress

GandR37.jpg ID 171314752 © Artinspiring | Dreamstime.com Religious leaders

GandR38.jpg ID 168865217 © Ekaterina Nikolaenko | Dreamstime.com Shaman in tribal mask

GandR39.jpg ID 117207915 © Maryna Kriuchenko | Dreamstime.com Moses Torah

GandR40.jpg ID 61916776 © Zcluars | Dreamstime.com Statue of Osiris and Isis with Horus

GandR41.jpg ID 163079323 © Ratpack2 | Dreamstime.com Queen Nofretete

GandR42.jpg ID 16504531 © Jeffrey Thompson | Dreamstime.com Mayan priest standing on slave

GandR43.jpg ID 19609860 © Philcold | Dreamstime.com Departure for the crusades

GandR44.jpg ID 178168664 © Vasyl Rogan | Dreamstime.com Torah scroll

GandR45.jpg ID 11164987 © Crafteepics | Dreamstime.com Crucifix and black Bible

GandR46.jpg ID 19511669 © Mohamed Osama | Dreamstime.com Holy Book of Quran

GandR47.jpg ID 141924627 © LakshmiPrasad lucky | Dreamstime.com The Holy Vedas

GandR48.jpg ID 144972904 © Samiramay | Dreamstime.com Witch books

GandR49.jpg ID 31946850 © Murali Nath | Dreamstime.com Indian Girl Praying

GandR50.jpg ID 65065081 © Dannyphoto80 | Dreamstime.com Child Muslim boy and girl praying

GandR51.jpg ID 123667567 © Nikhil Patil | Dreamstime.com Indian girl with lord Ganesha

GandR52.jpg ID 22896919 © Petr Novotny | Dreamstime.com The devils boiling the sinners

GandR53.jpg ID 178170030 © Eugenii Naumov | Dreamstime.com Different religions collection

GandR54.jpg ID 152944579 © Agus Wahyudi | Dreamstime.com World religion symbols

GandR55a.jpg ID215423254 © Vampy1| Dreamstime.com Ingenuity drone-helicopter in Mars

GandR55b.jpg ID 16068596 © Kyolhin | Dreamstime.com Biblical gathering

GandR56.jpg ID 2985876 © Chris Moncrieff | Dreamstime.com Wells Cathedral

GandR57.jpg ID 138908841 © Krzysztof Nahlik | Dreamstime.com Basilica of Our Lady of Licheń

GandR58.jpg ID 6163326 © Algirda Gelazius | Dreamstime.com Golden Temple in Myanmar

GandR59.jpg ID 140703791 © Leonid Andronov | Dreamstime.com Temple of Literature

GandR60.jpg ID 122321347 © Alexlibris | Dreamstime.com The Vegvisir, Icelandic symbols

GandR61.jpg ID 136426239 © Macrovector | Dreamstime.com Voodoo doll Mystique poster

GandR62.jpg ID 84197005 © Kalifer Art Creations | Dreamstime.com Satanism

GandR63.jpg ID 167563173 © Alexandra Barbu | Dreamstime.com Cosmic connection

GandR64.jpg ID 127269097 © Macrovector | Dreamstime.com Religious cult

GandR65.jpg ID |3743191 © Anticiclo | Dreamstime.com Marcus Aurelius

GandR66.jpg ID 132784554 © Artur Balytskyi | Dreamstime.com The solar system

ABOUT THE AUTHOR

Miguel Rosado has obsessed over the question of God and religions most of his life. He sees himself as a good person, so he does not accept the fate that he is being relegated by religions.

Printed in the United States
by Baker & Taylor Publisher Services